Crayfish Survey and Discovery of a Member of the *Cambarus acuminatus* complex (Decapoda: Cambaridae) at Valley Forge National Historical Park in Southeastern Pennsylvania

Technical Report NPS/NER/NRTR—2007/084

David A. Lieb[1], Robert F. Carline[2], and V. Malissa Mengel[3]

[1]Intercollege Graduate Degree Program in Ecology
The Pennsylvania State University
435 Forest Resources Building
University Park, Pennsylvania 16802
(dal105@psu.edu)

[2]Pennsylvania Cooperative Fish and Wildlife Research Unit
U.S.G.S. Biological Resources Division
The Pennsylvania State University
402 Forest Resources Building
University Park, Pennsylvania 16802

[3]Current address:
Tennessee Tech University
1100 North Dixie Avenue
205 Pennebaker Building
Cookeville, Tennessee 38505

June 2007

U.S. Department of the Interior
National Park Service
Northeast Region
Philadelphia, Pennsylvania

The Northeast Region of the National Park Service (NPS) comprises national parks and related areas in 13 New England and Mid-Atlantic states. The diversity of parks and their resources are reflected in their designations as national parks, seashores, historic sites, recreation areas, military parks, memorials, and rivers and trails. Biological, physical, and social science research results, natural resource inventory and monitoring data, scientific literature reviews, bibliographies, and proceedings of technical workshops and conferences related to these park units are disseminated through the NPS/NER Technical Report (NRTR) and Natural Resources Report (NRR) series. The reports are a continuation of series with previous acronyms of NPS/PHSO, NPS/MAR, NPS/BSO-RNR, and NPS/NERBOST. Individual parks may also disseminate information through their own report series.

Natural Resources Reports are the designated medium for information on technologies and resource management methods; "how to" resource management papers; proceedings of resource management workshops or conferences; and natural resource program descriptions and resource action plans.

Technical Reports are the designated medium for initially disseminating data and results of biological, physical, and social science research that addresses natural resource management issues; natural resource inventories and monitoring activities; scientific literature reviews; bibliographies; and peer-reviewed proceedings of technical workshops, conferences, or symposia.

Mention of trade names or commercial products does not constitute endorsement or recommendation for use by the National Park Service.

This report was accomplished under Cooperative Agreement 4000-3-2012, with assistance from the NPS. The statements, findings, conclusions, recommendations, and data in this report are solely those of the author(s), and do not necessarily reflect the views of the U.S. Department of the Interior, National Park Service.

Print copies of reports in these series, produced in limited quantity and only available as long as the supply lasts, or preferably, file copies on CD, may be obtained by sending a request to the address on the back cover. Print copies also may be requested from the NPS Technical Information Center (TIC), Denver Service Center, PO Box 25287, Denver, CO 80225-0287. A copy charge may be involved. To order from TIC, refer to document D-095.

This report may also be available as a downloadable portable document format file from the Internet at http://www.nps.gov/nero/science/.

Please cite this publication as:

Lieb, D. A., R. F. Carline, and V. M. Mengel. 2007. Crayfish Survey and Discovery of a Member of the *Cambarus acuminatus* complex (Decapoda: Cambaridae) at Valley Forge National Historical Park in Southeastern Pennsylvania. Technical Report NPS/NER/NRTR—2007/084. National Park Service. Philadelphia, PA.

NPS D-095   June 2007

Table of Contents

Tables

Figures

Abstract

The *Cambarus acuminatus* complex is a poorly known group of crayfish species whose range has traditionally been assumed to extend from the Patapsco River drainage in Maryland southward to the Saluda River basin in South Carolina. During a recent survey of Valley Forge National Historical Park in southeastern Pennsylvania, we collected a species of crayfish (*Cambarus* [*Puncticambarus*] sp. C) belonging to the *C. acuminatus* complex from Valley Creek. Collections were made from several habitats (pools, riffles, lateral areas, main-channel areas) in the spring and fall of 2003. Dominant substrate classes (e.g., cobble), current velocity, and depth were recorded along transects in each sampling area. We also re-examined specimens collected three years earlier from Valley Creek within Valley Forge National Historical Park by Jan Briede (Scientech, NES, Inc.) and Jamie Krejsa (Enviroscience, Inc.), and concluded that they were also *C.* (*P.*) sp. C. These collections are noteworthy because they represent a new crayfish record for the state of Pennsylvania and the first documented occurrence of any member of the *C. acuminatus* complex north of the Patapsco River basin. Of further interest, no member of the subgenus *Puncticambarus*, which includes the *C. acuminatus* complex, had previously been found in eastern Pennsylvania. Life history characteristics (e.g., sex ratio) of the population of *C.* (*P.*) sp. C inhabiting Valley Creek are provided and their variation among habitats and seasons is discussed. In pools, *C.* (*P.*) sp. C density was negatively related to current velocity, depth, and % sand, and positively related to % silt. In riffles, *C.* (*P.*) sp. C density was negatively related to current velocity. Comparisons among habitats indicated that *C.* (*P.*) sp. C was abundant in shallow, lateral areas but was scarce in main-channel areas. Although main-channel areas tended to have faster current, greater depth, more sand, and less silt than lateral areas, other factors could have been responsible for the relative scarcity of *C.* (*P.*) sp. C in the main channel. More conclusively, there was a positive relationship between the density of *C.* (*P.*) sp. C and % cobble in the main-channel areas of pools, suggesting that activities such as road construction and development, which result in sediment deposition and burial of rocky substrates, may have a negative effect on the density of *C.* (*P.*) sp. C in the main channel. Since main-channel areas are particularly important for large, reproductively mature individuals; reduced density in the main channel may affect the reproductive potential of the population. These findings indicate that Valley Creek within Valley Forge National Historical Park supports an unusual and potentially threatened crayfish population that requires further study and highlights the need for additional fieldwork in the region.

Acknowledgments

John Karish's support throughout this project was much appreciated. Thanks also go to Nellie Bhattarai, Brian Lambert (deceased), Adam Smith, and Paula Mooney for their contributions to this study. Raymond W. Bouchard, Ted R. Nuttall, Eric S. Long, John F. Karish, Matt M. Marshall, Margaret A. Carfioli, Jim Comiskey, and Carolyn Davis provided helpful critiques of the report. James L. Rosenberger provided statistical advice. We also thank John E. Cooper and Raymond W. Bouchard for verifying our identifications and for many informative discussions regarding the *C. acuminatus* complex. Lastly, we thank Jan Briede and Jamie Krejsa for collecting four unusual crayfish from Valley Creek in 2000 and Roger F. Thoma for recognizing that they belonged to the *C. acuminatus* complex, providing the impetus for this study.

Introduction

The *Cambarus acuminatus* complex is a poorly known group of crayfish species whose range has traditionally been assumed to extend from the Patapsco River drainage in Maryland southward to the Saluda River basin in South Carolina (Hobbs 1989). Published accounts of the complex are limited to collections from Maryland, Virginia, North Carolina, and South Carolina (Meredith and Schwartz 1960; Hobbs 1972, 1989; Taylor et al. 1996). Although the complex has not been previously reported from Pennsylvania, much of what is known about the state's crayfish fauna is dated and includes relatively few records from parts of southern Pennsylvania (see Ortmann [1906] and Schwartz and Meredith [1960]), where members of the complex are most likely to be found. In particular, large areas of southeastern Pennsylvania have never been sampled for crayfish.

Although considerable taxonomic progress has been made in recent years with the southern members of the complex, including the description of four new species from North Carolina (Cooper 2001; Cooper and Cooper 2003; Cooper 2006a, 2006b), northern populations remain virtually unknown (North Carolina State Museum of Natural Sciences [NCMNS], J. E. Cooper, Curator of Crustaceans, pers. comm., 2005). In fact, published information concerning the northern populations is currently limited to that provided by Meredith and Schwartz (1960), who reported *C. acuminatus* from 18 lotic sites located along the fall line (the transitional zone between the Piedmont and Coastal Plain) between Baltimore, Maryland and Washington, DC., but provided no additional information concerning the ecology of the species.

In early spring 2000, Jan Briede (Scientech, NES, Inc.) and Jamie Krejsa (Enviroscience, Inc.) collected four unusual crayfish specimens from Valley Creek within Valley Forge National Historical Park (VFNHP) in southeastern Pennsylvania. Those specimens were tentatively assigned to the *C. acuminatus* complex by Roger F. Thoma (Ohio State University Museum). If the identifications are confirmed, they represent the northern-most occurrence of the complex in the United States. As with other northern locations where members of the *C. acuminatus* complex have been found, almost nothing is known about the crayfish fauna of Valley Creek.

Because land use changes (e.g., urbanization) and associated sedimentation and habitat alterations threaten all the biota of Valley Creek (Kemp and Spotila 1997) and are problematic for crayfishes in general (see discussions in DiStefano et al. [2003a] and Westhoff et al. [2006]), it is essential that data regarding the creek's crayfish fauna be acquired so that informed decisions can be made about how to protect these animals. Management decisions must be based on the best possible information because not only do they have the potential to effect the future of Valley Creek's crayfish fauna, but also that of a possible species of concern in Pennsylvania, the queen snake (*Regina septemvittata*). The queen snake, which is found along Valley Creek within VFNHP, is thought to be disappearing from parts of Pennsylvania (particularly the southeastern part of the state) due to the adverse effects of pollution on its primary food source, crayfish (Hulse et al. 2001). Urbanization is not the only threat to Valley Creek's crayfish fauna. In fact, exotic crayfish (e.g., rusty crayfish [*Orconectes rusticus*]) are potentially an even greater concern, because they have been identified as one of the biggest threats to native crayfish in North America (Butler et al. 2003) and are abundant in several nearby streams, some of which are completely devoid of native crayfish (D. A. Lieb, The Pennsylvania State University [PSU], unpublished [unpubl.] data).

Although this study is of obvious regional and taxonomic significance, the ecological information (e.g., size structure and habitat preferences) provided in this paper should appeal to a much broader audience because, although crayfish often have major direct and indirect effects on the structure and function of rivers and streams (e.g., Huryn and Wallace 1987; Hart 1992; Creed 1994; Rabeni et al. 1995; Usio 2000; Schofield et al. 2001; Stenroth and Nyström 2003; Creed and Reed 2004), the life histories and habitat preferences of most species are unknown and are badly needed (Corey 1988; Taylor et al. 1996; Riggert et al. 1999; Hobbs 2001; DiStefano et al. 2003a; Westhoff et al. 2006). The objectives of this study were to (1) determine if a reproducing population of crayfish belonging to the *C. acuminatus* complex occurs in Valley Creek within VFNHP; (2) conduct a comprehensive survey of Valley Creek within VFNHP and produce a list of all the crayfish species that occur there; and (3) determine the basic life history characteristics (e.g., size structure, sex ratio), reproductive status, and habitat preferences of the crayfish species that occur in Valley Creek within VFNHP.

Valley Creek, which is located in the Piedmont of southeastern Pennsylvania, drains about 64 km² (40 mi²) of largely urbanized land in the Philadelphia suburbs. The creek consists of two main branches, Valley Creek and Little Valley Creek, which combine and then flow for about 5 km (3 mi) before emptying into the Schuylkill River (Figure 1). Four crayfish sampling stations were located in the lower reaches of Valley Creek within Valley Forge National Historical Park. GPS-based coordinates of the downstream limit of the sample stations were collected using a Trimble ProXRreceiver in datum NAD 83, UTM – zone 18. GPS files were differentially corrected and exported into ESRI ArcGIS shapefile format. Estimated accuracy of the points is 2 m (6.6 ft). Station 1, located downstream of the Wilson Road Bridge (easting 461294.326, northing 4436982.446), is the furthest upstream station. Station 4, located downstream of the Route 23 bridge (easting 460566.197, northing 4439071.051), is the furthest downstream station. Station 2 is located downstream of the covered bridge on Yellow Springs Road (easting 461063.124, northing 4437674.204). Station 3 (easting 461073.651, northing 4438338.403) is situated approximately midway between stations 2 and 4. Owing mainly to the presence of the park, our sampling stations are situated in what is perhaps the least disturbed section of the creek (Steffy and Kilham 2004). Because much of the creek's flow originates from limestone springs, temperatures tend to be moderate (4–18 °C [39–64 °F]), and nutrient availability is generally high (Sloto 1990). Additional information concerning Valley Creek and its biota are provided in Kemp and Spotila (1997).

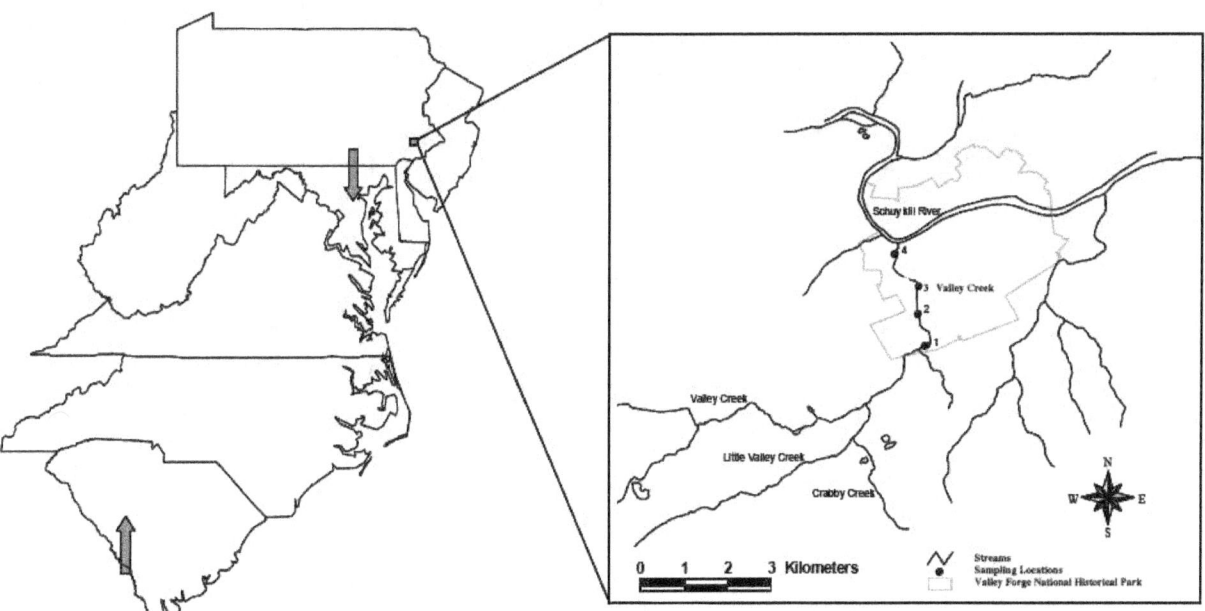

Figure 1. Map of the eastern United States from Pennsylvania to South Carolina with an enlargement of the study area. Valley Creek sampling locations are denoted by closed circles (●) and are numbered 1–4. Previous northern (tip of the down arrow) and southern (tip of the up arrow) limits of the *Cambarus acuminatus* complex are included on the map.

Methods

Crayfish Collections

We collected crayfish from four stations along Valley Creek within VFNHP (Figure 1). Each station consisted of one riffle-pool sequence and averaged 64 m (210 ft) in length (range=37–87 m [121–285 ft]). Within stations, stream widths averaged 14 m (46 ft [10–17 m {33–56 ft}]) for pools and 12 m (39 ft [6–18 m {20–59 ft}]) for riffles; bottom substrates were primarily cobble, gravel, sand, and silt. Large rocks (boulders), root masses, and aquatic vegetation were uncommon in most areas. At each station, crayfish samples were collected from four habitat types: shallow lateral areas of pools (SLP) and riffles (SLR) and main-channel areas of pools (MCP) and riffles (MCR). SL were within 2 m (6.5 ft) of shore. MC were ≥3 m (10 ft) from shore. Each station was sampled during daylight hours on two occasions: spring (21–22 April) and fall (18–19 October) of 2003. Sampling occurred during baseflow conditions when water clarity was high and the stream bottom was clearly visible.

Four collection techniques were employed during this survey. Seines (2.8×2.0 m bag seines with 5 mm mesh) were tried in the spring but not the fall because, as was found by Brant (1974), they often became snagged on various obstructions (e.g., cobbles) and were ineffective (0 crayfish collected). Rectangular traps (~0.2×0.3×0.6 m) were baited with raw beef kidney and placed overnight in pools and riffles at depths ranging from 0.3–1.2 m (12–47 in). Similar to the findings of Eng and Daniels (1982), Rabeni et al. (1997), and DiStefano (2000), traps were not useful in Valley Creek in the spring (a total of two crayfish captured during eight trap-nights) and were also not used in the fall. Dipnets (hand collections) were tried in the spring (a total of two crayfish captured) but were quickly abandoned because, similar to the results of Rabeni et al. (1997), they were ineffective (crayfish often missed) and inefficient over large reaches relative to electrofishing gear. Single-pass electrofishing was the primary collection method used during both the spring (347 individuals captured) and fall (262 individuals captured) and, as reported by Westman et al. (1978) and Rabeni et al. (1997), was effective in collecting crayfish from all the major habitats present at our sampling stations. The relative scarcity of large rocks, which for obvious reasons can be difficult to electrofish, likely contributed to the effectiveness of electrofishing gear in this study.

Electrofishing collections were made in an upstream direction using a boat-mounted unit (pulsed-DC current, 200-volt, Coffelt Electronics Company). Crayfish, which were often pulled out from under cover (e.g., cobbles, logs) during sampling, were involuntarily drawn to the anode (as described by Westman et al. [1978]) and netted. In most cases, four separate areas at each station (one area per habitat type) were sampled with electrofishing gear during each season. The physical characteristics of electrofished areas are listed in Table 1. Electrofishing data provided indices of crayfish density in each sampling area (individuals collected/m^2). Care was taken to ensure consistent effort among habitat types, seasons, and stations (especially in terms of the time spent sampling per unit of stream bottom).

Table 1. Physical characteristics of electrofished areas in Valley Creek, Valley Forge National Historical Park, Southeastern Pennsylvania. Mean values (±1SE) are reported for each habitat type (shallow lateral areas of riffles [SLR] and pools [SLP] and main-channel areas of riffles [MCR] and pools [MCP]) and were calculated by pooling data from the four sampling stations and two seasons (spring and fall). Sample sizes are provided in parentheses. Data were collected on 21–22 April and 18–19 October of 2003.

Habitat type	Depth (m)	Velocity (m/s)	Area (m^2)
SLR	0.12±0.02 (67)	0.11±0.03 (58)	67.2±19.2 (6)
SLP	0.26±0.02 (99)	0.05±0.01 (94)	126.1±13.8 (8)
MCR	0.23±0.01 (98)	0.51±0.03 (100)	156.8±46.0 (7)
MCP	0.45±0.02 (132)	0.17±0.01 (131)	297.1±40.2 (8)

In the spring, human error and electrofishing equipment failure prevented us from estimating density in some areas. For example, at station 1, specimens from SLR and MCR were inadvertently placed in the same jar, thereby preventing the calculation of separate density estimates for those locations. Additionally, electrofishing equipment failure prevented the collection of crayfish from SLR of station 2. Thus, in the spring, estimates of crayfish density were lacking for SLR of stations 1 and 2 and MCR of station 1.

After collection, crayfish were preserved in 95% ETOH and transported to our laboratory at The Pennsylvania State University where they were identified, and carapace length (CL[1]) and male reproductive state (Form I, II)[2] were determined. Females were inspected for eggs and young. Our species identifications were confirmed by John E. Cooper of the NCMNS and Raymond W. Bouchard of the Academy of Natural Sciences of Philadelphia. Voucher specimens were deposited in the crustacean collection of the NCMNS, Raleigh, North Carolina (catalogue numbers 24749–24753), the Ohio State University Museum, Columbus Ohio, and the Carnegie Museum of Natural History, Pittsburgh, Pennsylvania (catalogue numbers C2005-24-27). The remaining specimens are housed at The Pennsylvania State University.

Habitat Measurements

Dominant substrate classes (e.g., cobble), depth, and current velocity were recorded along transects within each electrofished area. Transects were oriented perpendicular to flow and were evenly spaced within each sampling area. In the spring, there were generally 5–6 transects per sampling area. Exceptions were the MCR of stations 2, 3 (no habitat data available), and 4 (only two transects). One set of habitat measurements (substrate, depth, flow) was made at the center of each transect. In the fall, there were 3–4 transects per sampling area. Within SL areas, measurements were made at locations ≤0.5, 1, and 2 m (1.6, 3, 6.5 ft) from shore along each transect. Within MC areas, 5–7 equally-spaced sets of measurements were made along each

---

[1]CL = the distance from the tip of rostrum to the posterior median margin of the carapace [see Figure 1 of Hobbs (1972)].

[2]The central projections of the first pleopod are corneous in form I (breeding) males; whereas they are not corneous in form II (non-breeding males) (see Hobbs 1972).

transect. Current velocity was measured at 0.6 of the distance from the water surface to the stream bottom using a portable flow meter (Marsh-McBirney Flow-mate 2000). Bottom substrates were assessed visually and the two dominant substrates recorded. Approximately 0.9 m^2 (3 ft^2) of stream bottom was assessed at each location. Substrates were assigned to size classes (e.g., silt, cobble) based on Platts et al. (1983).

Data Analysis

Electrofishing data were used to compare *C.* (*P.*) sp. C density between main habitats (pool vs. riffle) and sub-habitats (SL vs. MC) using a repeated measures, 4-factor (station, main habitat, sub-habitat, season), strip-plot ANOVA with station as a blocking factor (as described in Steel and Torrie [1980]). A repeated measures analysis (season terms included in the model) was used because the same areas were sampled on two occasions (spring and fall). A strip-plot (also called a split-block) design allowed us to account for the fact that, within each block, plots (pools, riffles) and subplots (SL, MC) were adjacent (see pg. 390 of Steel and Torrie [1980]). Station*main habitat*season and station*sub-habitat*season interaction terms could not be included in our model due to missing data (see 'Crayfish Collections' section of 'Methods'), which resulted in insufficient degrees of freedom. Thus, F-tests for sub-habitat*season and main habitat*season are approximate (but the best that can be done) because denominators consisted of the error mean square (MSE) instead of the more appropriate 3-way interaction (e.g., station*main habitat*season) mean square. Other F-tests were carried out as described in Steel and Torrie (1980).

Electrofishing data were also used to determine if there were relationships between *C.* (*P.*) sp. C density and microhabitat characteristics (current velocity, depth, % cobble, % sand, % silt, % gravel, % boulder) using correlation analysis. Since the primary objective of these analyses was to determine whether or not there was a relationship between microhabitat and density (regardless of the form of the relationship), we used Spearman's rank correlations (r_s) to test for associations between variables following Ott (1992) and Mendenhall and Beaver (1994). Because microhabitat measurements were made at multiple locations within each electrofished area, but only one density estimate was available for each area (the entire area was electrofished), microhabitat data were summarized prior to correlation analysis. For depths and current velocities, mean values were calculated. For substrate characteristics, the percent of locations where a particular substrate class (e.g., cobble) was dominant or co-dominant was determined.

Pools and riffles were analyzed separately for each microhabitat characteristic. MCP were of particular interest and were also analyzed separately because it appeared that those areas were often filled with fine sediments (silt, sand) of rather recent origin and therefore may be susceptible to sedimentation from ongoing urbanization of the watershed. Spring and fall data were pooled prior to analysis because relationships in the spring were similar to those in the fall, and sample sizes in individual seasons were relatively low.

More complicated and potentially more definitive microhabitat analyses (e.g., multiple regression) were not conducted because relationships between several of the microhabitat characteristics (e.g., % sand, current velocity) and density were confounded by the effects of sub-habitat (see 'Habitat Associations' section of 'Results and Discussion' for additional comments).

An obvious solution would be to analyze each sub-habitat type separately (e.g., separate multiple regressions for SLP, MCP, SLR, and MCR). Unfortunately, not enough data were available for separate analyses (Zar 1999). Additionally, simple correlations were adequate because the intent of our microhabitat analyses was to identify potentially important relationships to be explored further with additional data or experiments.

All *C*. (*P*.) sp. C specimens were used to compare size, sex ratio, and occurrence of form I males (male I) between seasons (e.g., size in spring vs. size in fall) and habitats (e.g., size in pools vs. size in riffles). Male and female size was also compared. Size comparisons were completed using a repeated measure, strip-plot ANOVA with station as a blocking factor (described previously). An additional factor (sex) was included to compare male and female size. Three-way interaction terms could not be included in the model due to missing data and the collection of only one sex from some locations, which resulted in insufficient degrees of freedom. Thus, F-tests for all 2-way interaction terms are approximate (but the best that can be done) because denominators for those tests consisted of the MSE instead of the more appropriate 3-way interaction terms (e.g., station*sub-habitat*season). Other F-tests were carried out as described in Steel and Torrie (1980). Mean sizes were used in these analyses because multiple crayfish were collected (and measured) from each sampling area. Means were weighted by the number of crayfish collected (n) because n varied among habitat types, stations, and seasons. Sex ratio and male I comparisons were carried out using chi-square tests.

Due to human error and equipment failure, size estimates were not available for some areas (the same areas which also lacked density estimates). Further, one *C*. (*P*.) sp. C could not be measured accurately or sexed (most of its abdomen missing) and was omitted from these analyses. An additional four specimens could also not be measured accurately due to damage and were not included in size analyses. For all analyses, p-values <0.05 were considered significant and Minitab Release 13 (Minitab, Inc., State College, Pennsylvania) was employed.

Results and Discussion

Taxonomy

Our surveys yielded two species of crayfish. One of those species, *Cambarus bartonii*, is common throughout much of the state, while the other, a member of the *C. acuminatus* complex (referred to as *C.* [*P.*] sp. C[3] after Hobbs and Peters [1977] and Cooper and Braswell [1995]), has never before been reported from Pennsylvania. Although we will not be able to assign a species name to the *C.* (*P.*) sp. C specimens until the complex is completely diagnosed (NCSMNS, J. E. Cooper, Curator of Crustaceans, pers. comm., 2005), they are almost certainly not true *C. acuminatus*, as originally described by Faxon (1884), because the native range of true *C. acuminatus* is likely limited to the Saluda River Basin in South Carolina (Hobbs 1969, NCSMNS, J. E. Cooper, Curator of Crustaceans, pers. comm., 2005). Additionally, the Valley Creek specimens are clearly not one of the four recently described species in the complex, and are therefore probably a new species that has not yet been described (NCSMNS, J. E. Cooper, Curator of Crustaceans, pers. comm., 2005).

Although one might argue that this report should wait until a species name can be attached to the Valley Creek specimens, that is likely many years away (NCSMNS, J. E. Cooper, Curator of Crustaceans, pers. comm., 2005), and preliminary data from ongoing surveys of southeastern Pennsylvania suggest that *C.* (*P.*) sp. C is probably native to Pennsylvania and, due to its limited range within the state and proximity to urban centers and populations of rusty crayfish, is highly threatened (Lieb et al. 2007). Thus, the data provided in this paper are needed to ensure the continued viability of one of the few populations of *C.* (*P.*) sp. C in Pennsylvania. Further, aside from a few *C. bartonii*, the specimens we have collected from Valley Creek are all the same species (NCSMNS, J. E. Cooper, Curator of Crustaceans, pers. comm., 2005) [i.e., we are not lumping multiple species under the name *C.* {*P.*} sp. C]). Thus, because we have properly cataloged a range of specimens at several museums, it will be possible, in the future, to attach a species name to our specimens and the information provided in this paper can then easily be attributed to that species. For additional information on the general morphology and taxonomy of crayfishes, the reader is referred to Ortmann (1906), Hobbs (1972), Page (1985), Hobbs (1989), Jezerinac et al. (1995), and Taylor and Schuster (2004).

Community Composition

Our surveys indicate that *C.* (*P.*) sp. C is the dominant crayfish species in Valley Creek. Of the 613 crayfish specimens collected during the 2003 surveys, 603 were *C.* (*P.*) sp. C, nine were *C. bartonii*, and one could not be identified to species (appeared to share characteristics of the two species, may have been a hybrid). The *C.* (*P.*) sp. C collections included large numbers of juveniles and adults (Figure 2), indicating that the species is established and is reproducing in Valley Creek. In contrast, although suitable habitat was available for *C. bartonii*, few were collected, making the reproductive status of this species in Valley Creek uncertain. In fact, it is possible that the *C. bartonii* collected from Valley Creek were washed in from upstream tributaries during rain events, which often result in rapid discharge increases in Valley Creek

---

[3]The four specimens collected in 2000 by Jan Briede (Scientech, NES, Inc.) and Jamie Krejsa (Enviroscience, Inc.) were re-examined and also found to be *C.* (*P.*) sp. C.

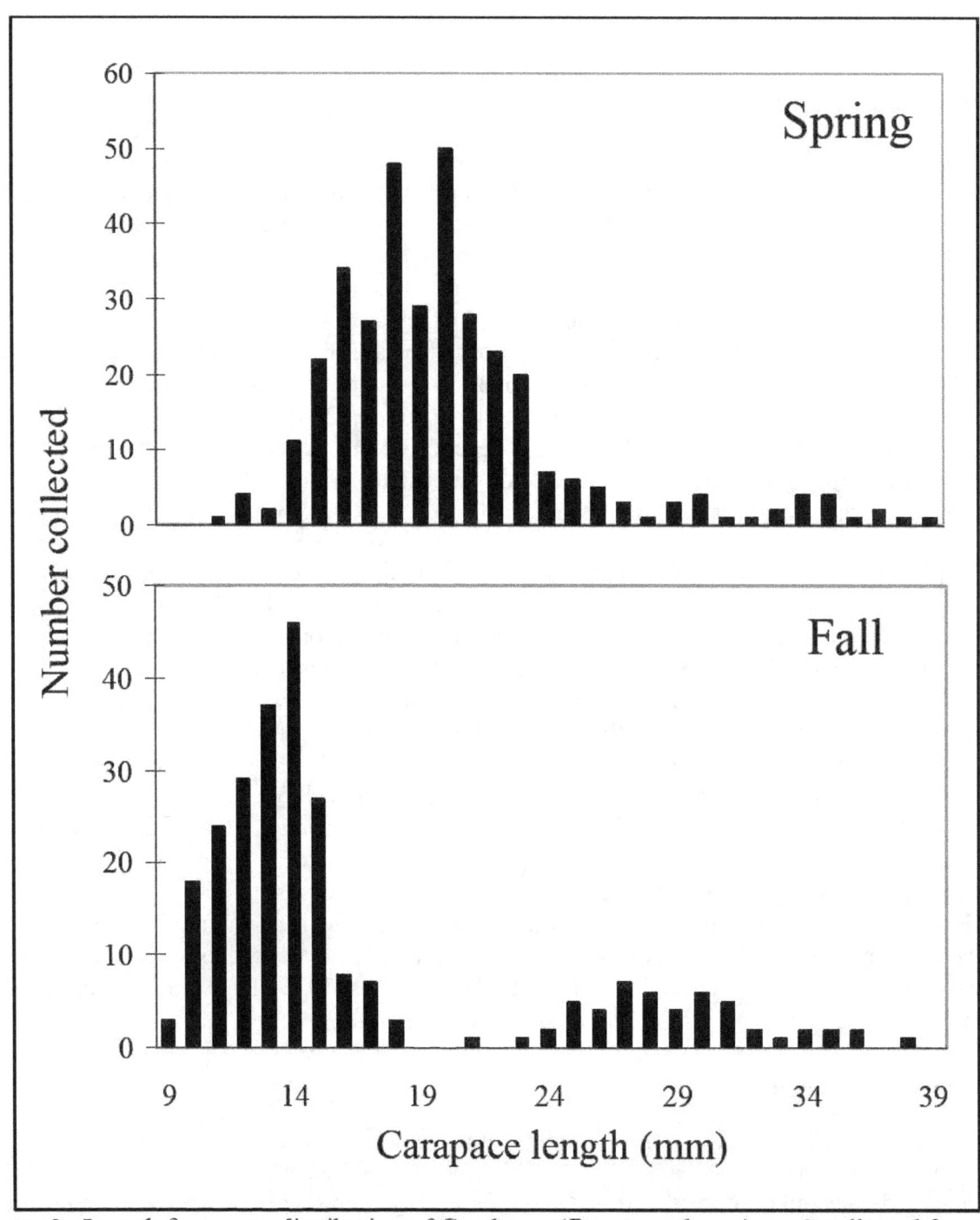

Figure 2. Length frequency distribution of *Cambarus* (*Puncticambarus*) sp. C collected from Valley Creek within Valley Forge National Historical Park in the spring (n=345, top panel) and fall (n=253, bottom panel) of 2003.

(United States Geological Survey [USGS] unpubl. streamflow data, gauging station 01473169, Valley Creek at Pennsylvania Turnpike Bridge near VFNHP). Additional information regarding the biology and distribution of *C. bartonii*, and crayfishes in general, can be found in Ortmann (1906), Hobbs (1972), Page (1985), Hobbs (1989), Jezerinac et al. (1995), and Taylor and Schuster (2004), and in the references listed in the 'Introduction' section.

Life History Characteristics

Size Structure

Although *C. (P.)* sp. C collections were devoid of females with attached ova or young (reproductive females), juveniles and adults of both sexes and all sizes were well represented. In both the spring and fall, it was evident that the size structure of the population was biased toward small individuals (>80% of the individuals collected were 9–23 mm carapace length [CL]) resulting in length-frequency distributions that are skewed to the left (Figure 2). An obvious break in the fall length-frequency histogram suggests the presence of at least two distinct size classes at that time (9–18 mm CL [peak at 14] and ~23–38 mm CL [peak at 27]). Size classes were less distinct in the spring, although peaks were observed at 18–20 mm CL and 30–35 mm CL. The presence of large numbers of very small (≤14 mm CL) individuals in the fall, but not the spring collections, suggests that substantial juvenile recruitment occurred sometime between the end of April and the end of October, which agrees with the general life history of many cambarid crayfishes (Hobbs 2001).

Males tended to be larger (least squares mean [LSM]=21.7 mm CL) than females (LSM=19.7 mm CL), as is often the case for crayfish (Reynolds 2002); however, differences were not significant (Table 2). This result was consistent across stations, sub-habitats, and main habitats, as indicated by the lack of significant interactions between sex and those factors. In contrast, we found a significant sex*season interaction, which was driven by the fact that males tended to be larger than females in one but not both seasons. Specifically, in the spring males were, on average, 22% larger than females (male LSM= 22.1 mm CL, female LSM=18.1 mm CL); whereas, in the fall male and female sizes were nearly identical (male LSM= 21.3 mm CL, female LSM=21.2 mm CL). Stated another way, male size was similar across seasons; whereas, females tended to be smaller in the spring than in the fall. These results are expected if large, mature females with attached ova and young, which are typically sequestered and difficult to collect (see subsequent 'Sex Ratio' and 'Gear Bias' sections of 'Results and Discussion'), were present in Valley Creek at the time of the April but not the October collections. The absence of large, reproductive females from the April collections would have reduced the average size of the females collected during that time. This explanation seems plausible given that, for cambarid crayfishes, females with attached eggs and young are typically present in spring but not fall (Hobbs 2001). Although these results make biological sense, the p-value for the season*sex interaction was not exceptionally small (0.02) and exact F-tests for interaction terms were not possible (see 'Data Analysis' section of 'Methods'), indicating that additional studies are needed to confirm the importance of sex*season interactions on *C. (P.)* sp. C size.

Table 2. Comparison of mean *Cambarus* (*Puncticambarus*) sp. C carapace length between main habitats (pool vs riffle), sub-habitats (lateral vs main channel), seasons (spring vs fall), and sexes (male vs female) using a repeated measures (season factor included), five factor, strip-plot (also called a split-block) ANOVA with station (1,2,3,4) as a blocking factor (as described in Steel and Torrie [1980]). A weighting factor (number of crayfish collected) was used because the number of individuals collected varied among locations. Three-way interaction terms could not be included in the model due to missing data and the collection of only one sex from some locations, which resulted in insufficient degrees of freedom. Thus, F-tests for all two-way interaction terms are approximate (but the best that can be done) because denominators for those tests consisted of the mean square error (MSE) instead of the more appropriate 3-way interaction terms (e.g., Station*Sub-habitat*Season). Other F-tests were carried out as described in Steel and Torrie (1980). *C.* (*P.*) sp. C were collected from Valley Creek within Valley Forge National Historical Park in 2003. Significant results in bold.

Source	d.f.	MS	F	P
Station	3	36.79	0.94	0.525
Main habitat	1	8.50	1.01	0.389
Station*Main habitat	3	8.40	0.16	0.919
Sub-habitat	1	1559.06	24.97	**0.015**
Station*Sub-habitat	3	62.45	1.23	0.326
Main habitat*Sub-habitat	1	184.28	3.64	0.071
Season	1	17.87	0.25	0.651
Station*Season	3	71.43	1.40	0.272
Main habitat*Season	1	0.03	0.00	0.979
Sub-habitat*Season	1	1132.91	22.27	**<0.001**
Sex	1	174.31	4.03	0.138
Station*Sex	3	43.29	0.85	0.483
Sub-habitat*Sex	1	11.62	0.23	0.639
Main habitat*Sex	1	206.17	4.04	0.059
Season*Sex	1	328.32	6.44	**0.020**
Error	19	51.09		

Differences in size were readily apparent among some, but not all habitat types. For example, main-channel areas supported much larger individuals (LSM=25.1 mm CL) than lateral areas (LSM=16.2 mm CL), but riffles and pools supported *C.* (*P.*) sp. C of similar size (pool LSM=20.3 mm CL, riffle LSM mean=21.0 mm CL) (Table 2). Although interaction terms should be interpreted cautiously, the sub-habitat*season interaction term was highly significant (p-value <0.001), indicating that the magnitude of the difference between sub-habitats (larger individuals in the main channel than in lateral areas) varied seasonally. More specifically, in the fall, individuals in the main channel were, on average, 93% larger than those in lateral areas (main channel LSM= 28.0 mm CL, lateral LSM=14.5 mm CL); whereas, in the spring, main-channel individuals were, on average, only 23% larger than those in lateral areas (main channel LSM= 22.2 mm CL, lateral LSM=18.0 mm CL). Phrased differently, individuals inhabiting main-channel areas were smaller in spring than fall; whereas in lateral areas individuals were larger in spring than fall. This interaction is probably best explained by the scarcity of large, reproductive females, which tend to prefer main-channel areas, in the spring collections (expected to result in reduced average size in the main channel) and/or the substantial influx of very small individuals, which tend to prefer lateral areas, in the fall (expected to result in reduced average size in lateral areas). In contrast, sub-habitat differences were consistent across stations, main habitats, and sexes, as indicated by the lack of significant interactions between sub-habitat and those factors. Similarly, main habitat results (no difference between pools and riffles) were consistent across stations, sub-habitats, seasons, and sexes, as indicated by the lack of significant interactions between main habitat and those terms.

There was a subtle trend toward the collection of smaller individuals at upstream compared to downstream stations; however, a significant station effect was not found (LSM for stations 1, 2, 3, and 4=18.6, 20.4, 20.4, and 23.3 mm CL, respectively) (Table 2). No significant interactions between station and the other factors were found indicating that size was similar across stations regardless of the main habitat, sub-habitat, season, or sex considered. Seasonal comparisons showed that size in the spring (LSM=20.1 mm CL) was not different from that in the fall (LSM=21.2 mm CL). Seasonal effects were consistent across stations and main habitats (station*season and main habitat*season were not significant), but varied among sub-habitats and sexes (sub-habitat*season and sex*season were significant).

Our finding that small individuals dominated collections of C. (P.) sp. C in Valley Creek is in agreement with studies of other crayfish species (e.g., Jordan et al. 1996; Englund and Krupa 2000; DiStefano et al. 2003a) and is not unexpected, given that crayfishes generally exhibit a type III (concave) survivorship curve with mortality decreasing markedly with age (size) (Hobbs 2001). Although we were able to roughly determine the timing of recruitment for C. (P.) sp. C in Valley Creek (sometime between the end of April and the end of October) and distinguish at least two size classes in each season (especially in the fall), a more complete determination of the life cycle of C. (P.) sp. C in Valley Creek would have required additional collections in other seasons (summer, winter) and at more frequent intervals (monthly or bimonthly), which was beyond the scope of this study.

While no data, other than that in this paper, are available concerning the size-habitat relationships of any member of the C. acuminatus complex, studies of other species tend to concur with our finding that deep, main-channel areas support larger individuals than shallow, lateral areas (Taylor 1983; Butler and Stein 1985; Rabeni 1985; Creed 1994; DiStefano et al. 2003a). Englund and Krupa (2000) explored the cause of this pattern and found that the distribution of small crayfish shifts to shallow water in the presence of fish predators. This result suggests that brown trout (Salmo trutta), which consume crayfish (Bachman 1991; Nyström et al. 2006; D. A. Lieb, PSU, unpubl. data) and are common in Valley Creek (Kemp and Spotila 1997), may be at least partly responsible for the tendency of small C. (P.) sp. C to occupy shallow, lateral areas in Valley Creek.

In contrast, much less is known about differences in crayfish size between pools and riffles, and few generalities are currently possible. In one of the few available studies, DiStefano et al. (2003a), who worked with an assemblage of crayfish composed mainly of Orconectes luteus, Orconectes ozarkae, and Orconectes punctimanus, showed that the ratio of adult density to young-of-the-year (YOY) density was much greater in riffles than in pools, indicating that crayfish CL was probably greater in riffles than in pools in their study. This result confirms

13

earlier, less direct work by Rabeni (1985), who found that *O. luteus* YOYs preferred low-velocity areas, whereas, adults preferred high-velocity areas; again suggesting that individual size in riffles (high-velocity areas) is greater than that in pools (low-velocity areas) for *O. luteus*. In contrast, Gore and Bryant (1990) found that YOY *Orconectes neglectus* preferred high-velocity areas with cobble (generally found in riffles), whereas adults preferred low-velocity, macrophyte beds (generally found in pools). Therefore, it seems likely that the size of individuals in pools is greater than that in riffles for *O. neglectus*. Thus, large individuals were concentrated in riffles for *O. luteus*, *O. ozarkae*, *O. punctimanus*, in pools for *O. neglectus*, and were spread equally among pools and riffles for *C.* (*P.*) sp. C., suggesting that, for crayfishes, there are species-specific differences in how juveniles and adults are distributed among certain habitat types (e.g., riffles and pools). These differences may be due to factors that are internal (innate, biological differences among species) or external (differences in the physical or biological characteristics of the communities in which the species live). For example, in some species, juveniles may be better equipped than adults to deal with the high flows that are common in riffles and, as a result, may be very abundant in those areas; whereas in other species, the opposite may be true (adults better able to deal with high flows than juveniles). Alternatively, juveniles of some crayfish species may avoid riffles to reduce the likelihood of contact with small, predatory fishes (e.g., madtoms [*Noturus*], sculpins [*Cottus*]; see DiStefano et al. 2003a), whereas juveniles of other species, which do not coexist with predatory, riffle-dwelling fishes, may freely colonize those areas.

Although the absence of reproductive females from our collections likely contributed to the interactions observed (sex*season, sub-habitat*season), other results were probably little affected. For example, the collection of reproductive females would, undoubtedly, have increased the average size of the individuals in the main channel (because reproductive individuals tend to be large, and large individuals prefer main-channel areas), strengthening our finding that individuals in the main channel are larger than those in lateral areas. This argument is based on several assumptions. First, we assume that reproductive females tend to be large, which is likely true, given that many cambarid crayfishes do not reach maturity until their second or even third year of life (e.g., Hamr and Berrill 1985; Corey 1988, Hobbs 2001). Second, we assume that large reproductive females are distributed similarly to large non-reproductive females (i.e., large reproductive females prefer main-channel areas). Anecdotal support for this assertion is provided by recent surveys of nearby streams, which resulted in the collection of a few reproductive female *C.* (*P.*) sp. C., all of which were found in main-channel areas (D. A. Lieb, PSU, unpubl. data).

Sex Ratio

Across seasons and habitat types, the sex ratio of *C.* (*P.*) sp. C was male-biased, although the bias was not extreme (1.2:1 [male:female], n=602, Chi-square test, p=0.01). When individual seasons or habitat types were considered, deviations from 1:1 were sometimes larger. For example, there was a male bias in the spring (1.4:1, n=348, p=0.002), but not the fall (1.02:1, n=254, p=0.90). Similarly, when habitats were considered individually, riffles were male-biased (1.4:1, n=201, p=0.02), whereas pools were not (1.1:1, n=401, p=0.18). Partitioning the data between main-channel and lateral areas showed a male bias in the main channel (1.6:1, n=91, p=0.03), but not in lateral areas (1.1:1, n=416, p=0.49)[4].

Although the sex ratios of most crayfish populations are believed to be 1:1 (Reynolds 2002), a number of authors have reported male-biased catches during at least part of the year (e.g., Fenouil and Chaix 1985; Van Den Brink et al. 1988; Ackefors 1999; Alekhnovich et al. 1999) and some attributed this bias to the use of a particular collection technique (e.g., trapping tends to be biased toward males). We also found that *C.* (*P.*) sp. C catches were male-biased during part of our study (in the spring but not the fall) and attribute this, at least in part, to the lack of reproductive females in our collections, but not to our choice of collection techniques (see 'Gear Bias' section of 'Results and Discussion').

The generality of our finding that sex ratios vary among habitats in Valley Creek (male bias in riffles and main-channel areas but not in pools and lateral areas) is unknown at this time because few data are available. However, variation in sex ratios among habitats in Valley Creek is not unexpected, given that the biology of male and female crayfish often differs, especially during the breeding season. For example, females often feed less than males during the egg-bearing stage of their reproductive cycle (Hopkins 1967; Abrahamsson 1971; Skurdal and Qvenild 1986; Pursiainen et al. 1987), which ultimately may result in males and females selecting habitats based on different criteria during parts of their life cycle (e.g., food availability may be a higher priority for males than females during egg-bearing). Alternatively, male-biased catches in particular habitats could have been due, at least in part, to difficulties in collecting reproductive females. For example, if reproductive females favored particular habitats (e.g. main-channel areas) but were deeply burrowed into the substrate and were inaccessible, then male-biased catches would be expected in those areas.

Form I Males

During this study, form I males only accounted for 7% of the total *C.* (*P.*) sp. C catch. The contribution of form I males to the catch was consistent across seasons (8% in the spring and 6% in the fall) (Chi-square test, p=0.42), but not habitats. For example, form I males accounted for a higher proportion of the catch in riffles (10%) than in pools (6%) (p =0.04), and a higher proportion of the catch in main-channel areas (26%) than in lateral areas (3%) (p<0.001). Form I males were particularly well represented in main-channel riffle collections, comprising 53% of the catch in those areas. However, overall abundance in those areas was low (only 19 of 603 *C.* [*P.*] sp. C were collected there).

Our finding that form I male *C.* (*P.*) sp. C comprised little of the total catch in Valley Creek was expected given the results of other studies. For example, of the >6,000 specimens belonging to five different species collected by Flinders and Magoulick (2005), <400 were form I males (<6% of the total catch). Studies by Corey (1988) and Riggert et al. (1999) with three other crayfish species also showed that form I males were rarely collected during some seasons.

---

[4]Ninety-five specimens were omitted from the lateral and main-channel analyses because sub-habitat data (e.g., main channel, lateral) were not available for those specimens (see 'Crayfish Collections' section of 'Methods').

Gear Bias

Although gear bias is a concern when studying the life history characteristics of any species and has the potential to affect crayfish collections, the results of Westman et al. (1978) and Rabeni et al. (1997) suggest that, unlike other collection methods which tend to be highly biased (e.g., traps favor large males; quadrant samplers favor juveniles), electrofishing is an effective method for collecting crayfish of all sizes and life stages (even reproductive females) from a variety of habitats, even where there is heavy cover. Westman et al. (1978) cautioned that electrofishing was not effective in murky waters or depths $\geq$0.8 m (2.6 ft); however, water clarity in Valley Creek was high throughout this study and depths $\geq$0.8 m (2.6 ft) were rarely encountered (only 3% of our depth measurements exceeded 0.8 m [2.6 ft]; Table 1). Based on this information, our own observations (see 'Methods'), and the fact that electrofishing gear has been used in similar studies of other large-bodied, freshwater crustaceans (e.g., Australian shrimps; Richardson and Cook 2006), it is tempting to conclude that electrofishing is completely unbiased. However, the fact remains that females with attached ova or young were not collected during this study, which may have biased our collections toward males (especially in the spring when reproductive females are expected).

Studies of other members of the *C. acuminatus* complex suggest that this bias likely had nothing to do with gear type and was probably due to the fact that female members of the complex are extremely difficult to catch during parts of their reproductive cycle. For example, despite extensive collections of the complex (four species, >800 individuals) from a variety of locations by a variety of collectors (presumably using a variety of sampling devices), only two females with attached young and one with attached ova have been reported from North Carolina (Cooper 2001; Cooper and Cooper 2003; Cooper 2006a, 2006b). Similar results (few reproductive females collected) for a number of other crayfish species collected using a variety of methods (e.g., dipnets, kicknets, quadrant samplers, hand collections; Fenouil and Chaix 1985; Hamr and Berrill 1985; Corey 1988; Flinders and Magoulick 2005) provide additional evidence that male-biased catches in Valley Creek were not due to the use of electrofishing gear.

Habitat Associations

Comparisons among habitats revealed that *C. (P.)* sp. C density was much higher in lateral (LSM=0.26 individuals/m^2) than in main-channel areas (LSM=0.02 individuals/m^2) (Table 3). Density of *C. (P.)* sp. C also tended to be higher in pools (LSM=0.17 individuals/m^2) than in riffles (LSM=0.10 individuals/m^2), but differences were not significant. Density of *C. (P.)* sp. C in the spring (0.16 individuals/m^2) was similar to that in the fall (0.12 individuals/m^2). *C. (P.)* sp. C density was also similar among stations (LSM for stations 1, 2, 3, and 4=0.15, 0.12, 0.16, and 0.13 individuals/m^2, respectively), suggesting that, at least within our study area, there is little longitudinal (upstream-downstream) variation in the abundance of this species. No significant interactions were found, indicating that these results were consistent across all habitats, seasons, and stations. Although few *C. (P.)* sp. C were found in the main channel, the individuals present were, on average, 55% larger than those found in lateral areas, suggesting that differences in biomass between main-channel and lateral areas may not be as large as differences in density.

Table 3. Comparison of *Cambarus* (*Puncticambarus*) sp. C density between main habitats (pool vs riffle), sub-habitats (lateral vs main channel), and seasons (spring vs fall) using a repeated measures (season factor included), four factor, strip-plot (also called a split-block) ANOVA with station (1,2,3,4) as a blocking factor (as described in Steel and Torrie [1980]). Station*Main habitat*Season and Station*Sub-habitat*Season interaction terms could not be included in the model due to missing data, which resulted in insufficient degrees of freedom. Thus, F-tests for Sub-habitat*Season and Main habitat*Season interaction terms are approximate (but the best that can be done) because denominators for those tests consisted of the mean square error (MSE) instead of the more appropriate 3-way interaction terms (e.g., Station*Sub-habitat*Season). Other F-tests were carried out as described in Steel and Torrie (1980). *C.* (*P.*) sp. C were collected from Valley Creek within Valley Forge National Historical Park in 2003. Significant results in bold.

Source	d.f.	MS	F	P
Station	3	0.002	0.19	0.912
Main habitat	1	0.027	0.96	0.399
Station*Main habitat	3	0.028	1.39	0.388
Sub-habitat	1	0.349	486.82	**<0.001**
Station*Sub-habitat	3	0.001	0.03	0.990
Main habitat*Sub-habitat	1	0.022	1.05	0.380
Station*Main habitat*Sub-habitat	3	0.021	2.06	0.193
Season	1	0.007	0.65	0.479
Station*Season	3	0.011	1.09	0.415
Main habitat*Season	1	0.000	0.04	0.849
Sub-habitat*Season	1	0.003	0.31	0.595
Error	7	0.010		

Although the density values reported above likely underestimated actual density because multiple electrofishing passes are typically required to collect all the crayfish from a given area (Westman et al. 1978; Rabeni et al. 1997; D. A. Lieb, PSU, unpubl. data), comparisons among habitats, seasons, and stations were probably little affected by this bias because our sampling procedures were consistent throughout the study (particularly in terms of effort). Our finding that *C.* (*P.*) sp. C density in lateral areas was much greater than that in the main channel was probably particularly robust to any such bias because smaller-scale, more intensive studies elsewhere in Pennsylvania indicate that additional electrofishing passes (beyond the initial pass) substantially increase the catch of small crayfish (particularly in lateral areas; D. A. Lieb, PSU, unpubl. data). Thus, actual differences in density between lateral and main channel areas were likely even greater than those we documented. More generally, our densities can be thought of as catch-per-unit-effort values (CPUE; effort standardized by the area sampled and time), which are measures of abundance that have been successfully used to determine habitat preferences in a wide range of aquatic species (e.g, Lazzari et al. 2003; Barko and Hrabik 2004; Jordan et al. 2004; and Wallace and Hartman 2006). Additional multiple-pass removal studies in Valley Creek may allow our values to be converted to actual densities in the future (by determining the % of the total population that is captured during the first pass).

Substrate analyses revealed that there was a positive relationship between $C.$ $(P.)$ sp. C density and the prevalence of cobble (% cobble) in main-channel areas of pools (r_s=0.76, p<0.05; Figure 3). Relationships between other substrate characteristics (% sand, % silt, % gravel, % boulder) and density were not significant. When main-channel and lateral data were combined, there was a negative relationship between density and % sand (r_s= −0.57, p<0.05; Figure 4) and a positive relationship between density and % silt (r_s=0.62, p<0.05) in pools. Relationships between other substrate characteristics (% gravel, % cobble, % boulder) and density were not significant. Analyses with riffle data (main-channel and lateral data combined) did not reveal any significant relationships between density and any substrate characteristic.

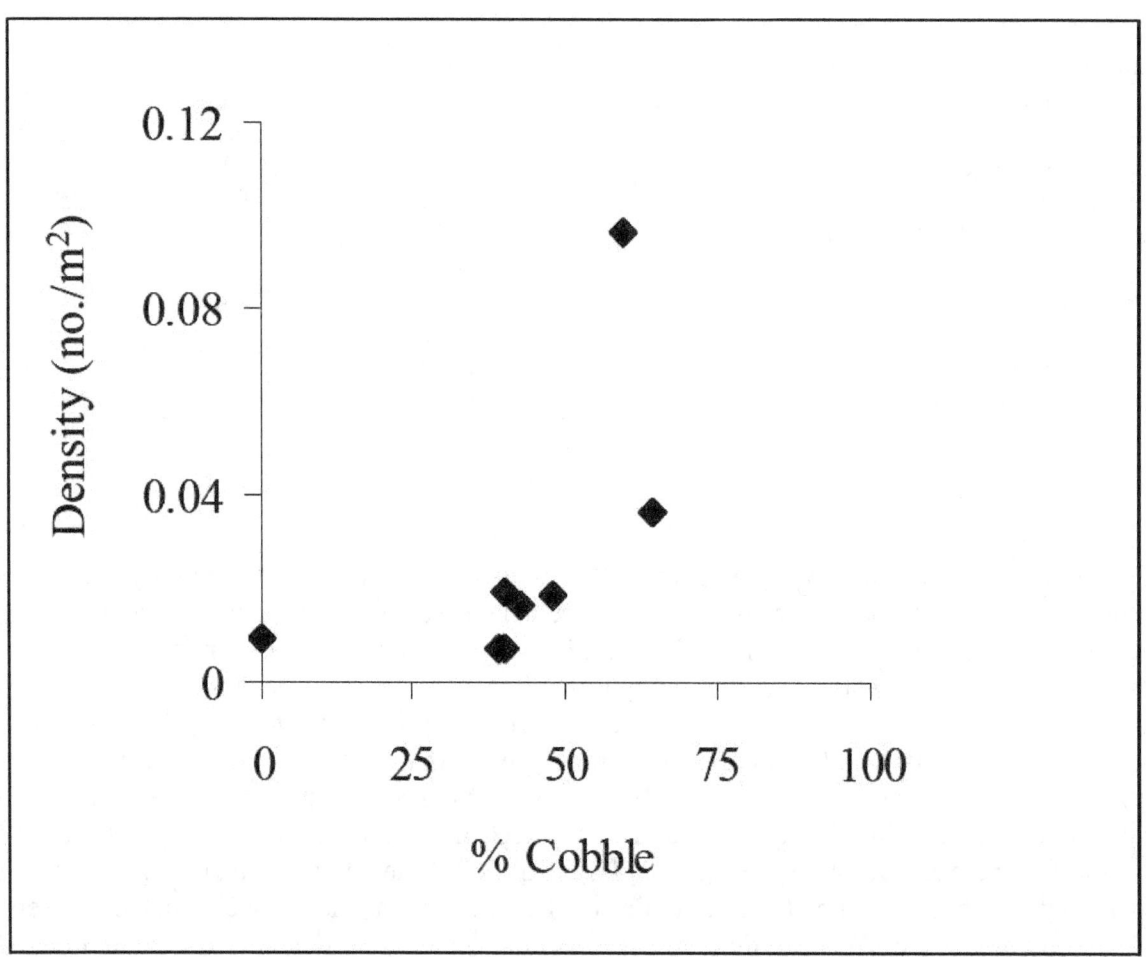

Figure 3. Relationship between the % of the sampling area where cobble was either the dominant or co-dominant substrate type (% cobble) and *Cambarus* (*Puncticambarus*) sp. C density (no./m^2) in main-channel areas of pools. Samples were collected from Valley Creek within Valley Forge National Historical Park in spring and fall of 2003.

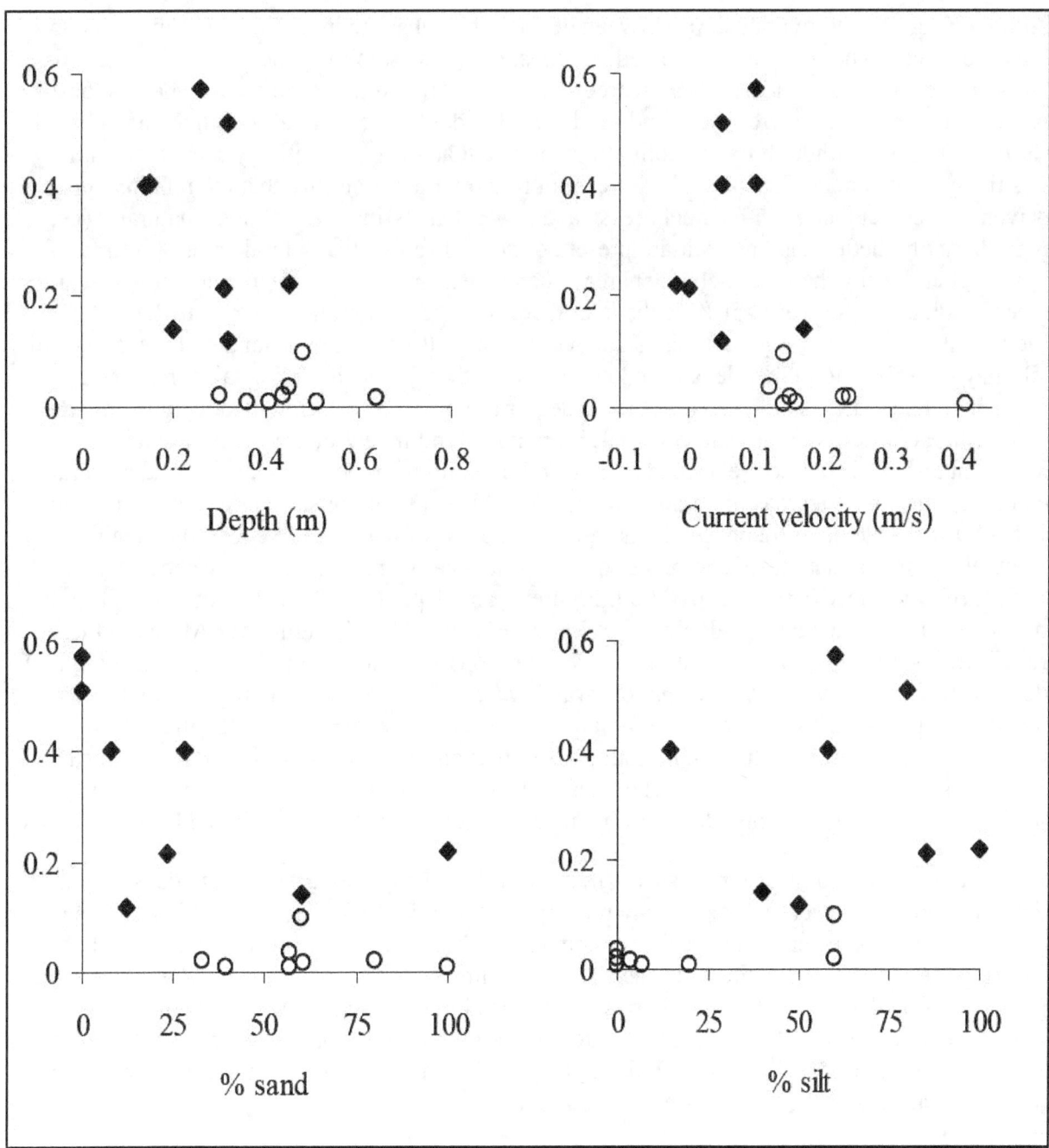

Figure 4. Relationship between depth (upper left), current velocity (upper right), substrate characteristics and *Cambarus* (*Puncticambarus*) sp. C density (no./m²) in lateral (♦) and main-channel (o) areas of pools. Substrate characteristics were calculated as the percent of the sampling area where sand (% sand, lower left) or silt (% silt, lower right) was the dominant or co-dominant substrate type. Samples were collected from Valley Creek within Valley Forge National Historical Park in spring and fall of 2003.

Although significant, relationships between density and substrate in pools (main-channel and lateral data combined) should be viewed cautiously because sampling locations where crayfish and silt were abundant and sand was scarce were mainly found in lateral areas, whereas locations where crayfish and silt were scarce and sand was abundant were generally in the main channel (Figure 4). Thus, although it is tempting to conclude that sand is negatively related and silt positively related to density in pools, we cannot rule out the possibility that the relationship is driven by the fact that main-channel areas have lower density than lateral areas naturally (i.e., regardless of whether sand and silt are present or not). The fact that lateral areas appeared to have higher density than main-channel areas even when sand was abundant and silt was scare (see two data points where >50% of the lateral areas are sand and one data point where <15% of the lateral area is silt in Figure 4) suggests that, although the absence of sand and prevalence of silt may contribute to higher density in lateral areas, other factors are likely also important. Experimental studies (sand and silt either added or removed) or additional collections in main-channel areas where sand is scarce and silt is abundant and in lateral areas where sand is abundant and silt is scarce are needed to clarify the relationship between density and substrate characteristics in pool areas of Valley Creek. There was no relationship between density and either current velocity or depth in the main-channel areas of pools. However, when main-channel and lateral data were combined, there was a negative relationship between density and both current velocity ($r_s=-0.72$, $p<0.005$; Figure 4) and depth ($r_s=-0.58$, $p<0.05$) in pools and between density and current velocity in riffles ($r_s=-0.81$, $p<0.005$; Figure 5). Although these relationships are strong, they should be viewed cautiously because sampling locations with high density, low current velocity, and shallow water were mainly found in lateral areas, whereas locations with low density, high velocity, and deep water were generally in the main channel (Figures 4, 5). Thus, the situation is analogous to that discussed previously for sand and silt. Regardless, *C.* (*P.*) sp. C was completely absent from areas where average flows exceeded about 0.50 m/s, suggesting that some fast-current areas of Valley Creek are unsuitable for this species.

Within our study area, we found a strong negative relationship between crayfish density and depth in pools; however, this result may not apply to all areas of Valley Creek. This is because relationships between crayfish density and depth may be affected by the presence of predatory fish (e.g., brown trout) and, in some cases, relationships may shift from strongly negative in the presence of predatory fish to strongly positive in the absence of predatory fish (Englund 1999). Therefore, in reaches of Valley Creek where brown trout are rare (upstream, headwater areas; Kemp and Spotila [1997]) we may find a different relationship than we found in downstream locations where brown trout are common (our study area).

Although *C.* (*P.*) sp. C is abundant in the lateral areas of Valley Creek, where the water is shallow, current velocity is low, sand is scarce, and silt is abundant, our results can only suggest associations and cannot determine causality. This is because any number of other factors, such as the prevalence of food resources (e.g., detritus, small invertebrates) and woody debris in lateral areas or the presence of predatory fish (brown trout) in main-channel areas could have been responsible for the macro-habitat associations observed (see Rabeni [1985] and DiStefano et al. [2003a] for thorough discussions of many of these possibilities). Given the flashy nature of Valley Creek, root masses, which occur in lateral areas, may also be important, because tree roots afford some crayfish species protection from floods (Smith et al. 1996).

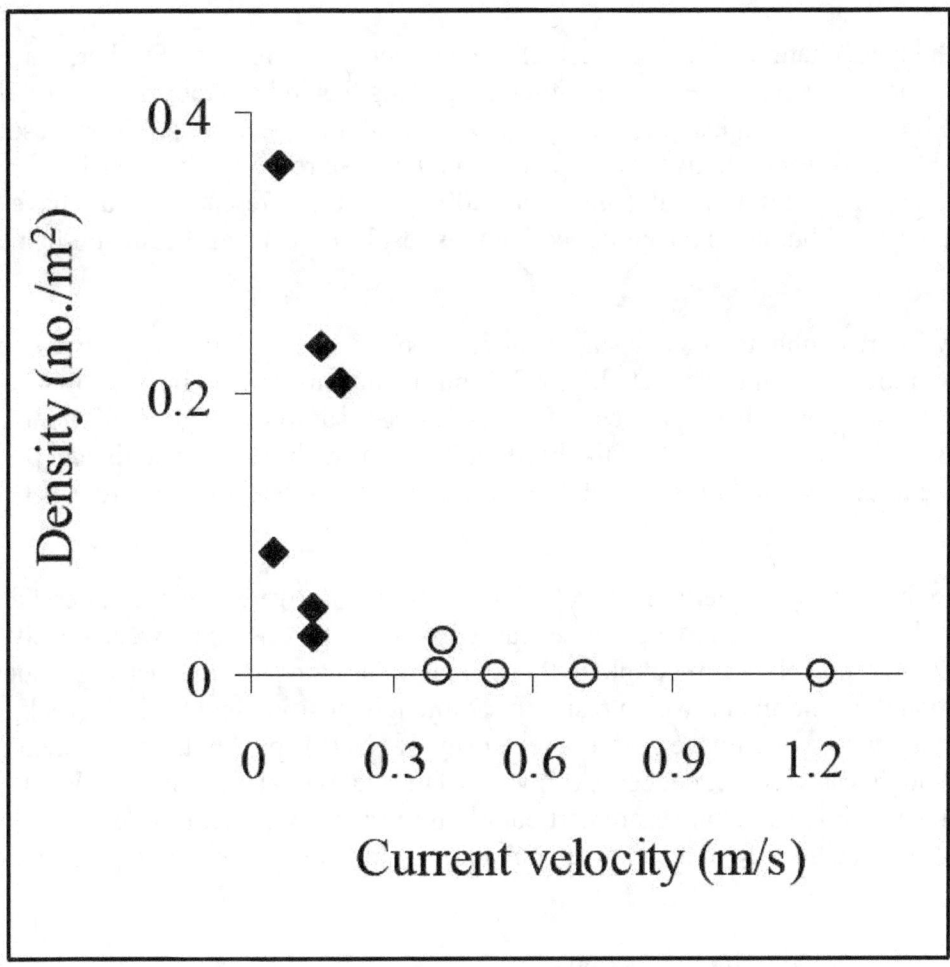

Figure 5. Relationship between current velocity and *Cambarus* (*Puncticambarus*) sp. C density (no./m^2) in lateral ($\blacklozenge$) and main-channel (o) areas of riffles. Samples were collected from Valley Creek within Valley Forge National Historical Park in spring and fall of 2003.

Whatever the cause, it is clear that *C*. (*P*.) sp. C density was much higher in shallow, lateral areas than in the main channel during both the spring and the fall sampling periods and that this difference in density was primarily driven by the preference of small individuals (which dominated our collections) for shallow, lateral areas. This result adds to a growing list of stream-dwelling crayfishes, which, as juveniles, show a distinct preference for shallow, lateral areas (Butler and Stein 1985; Creed 1994; DiStefano et al. 2003a).

One might argue that the lack of reproductive females in our collections reduced densities in the main channel relative to lateral areas (because reproductive females are expected to select main-channel areas); however, their absence certainly did not result in differences in density as large as we observed (> an order of magnitude). This is because crayfishes are characterized by high juvenile mortality with few individuals surviving to reproductive age (Hobbs 2001). Thus, the absence of reproductive females, which probably account for a minor proportion of overall density in the main channel, likely had a negligible affect on our results. Further, our finding that lateral densities were greater than main-channel densities in both the spring and fall (sub-habitat*season interaction not significant [p=0.595]) would not be expected if our results were due to the absence of reproductive females. Instead, because reproductive females should be present in the spring but not the fall (see Hobbs 2001), habitat differences should have been apparent in the April but not the October collections resulting in a significant sub-habitat*season interaction.

Although we were unable to detect a statistical difference in crayfish density between pools and riffles, as was found by DiStefano et al. (2003b), our results are qualitatively similar to theirs (higher densities in pools than in riffles). The much larger sampling effort (>60 × more samples collected) of DiStefano et al. (2003b) likely provided them with far more statistical power than we were able to achieve and thus a much higher probability of detecting differences between pools and riffles.

Although we cannot say for certain why *C.* (*P.*) sp. C densities were higher in lateral areas than in the main channel, we do know that there was a positive relationship between density in main-channel areas and prevalence of cobble in those areas. This suggests that activities such as road construction and development, which result in sediment deposition and burial of rocky substrates, may have a negative effect on the density of *C.* (*P.*) sp. C in the main channel (see similar, although less specific, concerns echoed by DiStefano et al. [2003a] and Westhoff et al. [2006]). Since main-channel areas are particularly important for large, reproductively mature individuals, reduced density in the main channel may affect the reproductive potential of the population.

Conservation Status and Future Directions

The discovery of a reproducing population of *C.* (*P.*) sp. C in Valley Creek is noteworthy because it is the first documented occurrence of any member of the *C. acuminatus* complex north of the Patapsco River basin in Maryland (Figure 1), and, as such, represents a new crayfish record for Pennsylvania. Of further interest, no member of the subgenus *Puncticambarus*, which includes the *C. acuminatus* complex, had previously been found in eastern Pennsylvania. Although efforts to determine the range of *C.* (*P.*) sp. C in Pennsylvania are not yet complete, preliminary results suggest that it is likely restricted to Valley Creek and several nearby streams, and is probably native to Pennsylvania (D. A. Lieb, PSU, unpubl. data). Similar studies in neighboring states, where members of the *C. acuminatus* complex are known to occur (e.g., Maryland, Virginia), are needed to determine the complete range of the species. The conservation status of the species depends critically on this information because, if it is a narrow endemic that is found only in southeastern Pennsylvania, then it may be threatened on the federal level; however, if it has a broader distribution that includes locations in other states, then it may only be threatened on the state level. Regardless, because *C.* (*P.*) sp. C is only known from a few locations in Pennsylvania, all of which are threatened by urbanization and rusty crayfish (D. A. Lieb, PSU, unpubl. data), regulatory action may be necessary to prevent its extirpation from the state.

Conclusions and Management Recommendations

This study revealed that Valley Creek within VFNHP supports a crayfish species (C. [P.] sp. C), which had not previously been reported from Pennsylvania. Although the complete distribution of the species awaits additional survey work in other nearby states (Maryland, Virginia), this study, along with preliminary results from other ongoing surveys of Pennsylvania, suggests that the species is probably native to Pennsylvania and has a narrow distribution within the state (D. A. Lieb, PSU, unpubl. data). Thus, it seems likely that C. (P.) sp. C is one of the most threatened aquatic species in Pennsylvania, although its conservation status at the federal level is unknown. Regardless, because C. (P.) sp. C is only known from a few streams in Pennsylvania, all of which are threatened by urbanization and rusty crayfish (D. A. Lieb, PSU, unpubl. data), regulatory action may be necessary to prevent its extirpation from the state.

Based on this information, it is clear that VFNHP represents an important strong-hold for C. (P.) sp. C in Pennsylvania. Unfortunately, it seems unlikely, given ongoing threats from exotic species (rusty crayfish), that Valley Creek's population of C. (P.) sp. C can be maintained without proactive strategies to protect it. More specifically, programs aimed at educating the public about the dangers of moving crayfish from one water body to another are needed to prevent introductions of exotic crayfish into Valley Creek. The establishment of signs along the creek warning the public not to release crayfish into the water are also needed. These measures are particularly important because Valley Creek is a well-established recreational fishery, and exotic crayfish are often spread through bait-bucket introductions (Lodge et al. 2000). Further, exotic crayfish are extremely difficult to extirpate once they become established (particularly rusty crayfish); thus, preventive measures (such as those mentioned above) are essential if the population of C. (P.) sp. C inhabiting Valley Creek is to be preserved.

Because of its location in the suburbs of Philadelphia, urbanization and resulting habitat alterations and influx of toxic chemicals and sediment also represent a significant threat to Valley Creek's aquatic resources, including C. (P.) sp. C (Kemp and Spotila 1997; Lieb and Carline 1999, 2000). Thus, although efforts to mitigate the effects of urbanization on Valley Creek are likely needed to ensure the preservation of C. (P.) sp. C, such efforts, and their potential effect on C. (P.) sp. C, should be considered carefully prior to being enacted. Similarly, any management activities that have the potential to effect Valley Creek's population of C. (P.) sp C. should be thoroughly evaluated before being implemented.

Given these ongoing threats to Valley Creek, it would seem prudent to periodically survey the crayfish community of the creek. Because of this baseline data, future surveys would allow park officials to monitor the status of the population of C. (P.) sp C inhabiting the creek. These surveys would provide additional benefits by allowing park officials to detect and potentially eliminate exotic crayfish before they become well-established. If exotic crayfish are discovered in Valley Creek, local bait shops could also be visited in an effort to determine the source of the exotics. If bait shops are selling exotic crayfish, then those operations could be halted (it is currently illegal to sell or possess rusty crayfish in PA), helping to prevent future introductions.

Literature Cited

Abrahamsson, S. A. 1971. Density, growth and reproduction of the crayfish *Astacus astacus* and *Pacifastacus leniusculus*. Oikos 22:373–88.

Ackefors, H. E. G. 1999. Observations on the yearly life cycle of *Astacus astacus* in a small lake in Sweden. Freshwater Crayfish 12:413–29.

Alekhnovich, A., V. Kulesh, and S. Ablov. 1999. Growth and size structure of the narrow-clawed crayfish, *Astacus leptodactylus* (Esch), in its eastern area. Freshwater Crayfish 12:550–554.

Bachman, R. A. 1991. Brown trout (*Salmo trutta*), pp. 208–229. *In* J. Stolz and J. Schnell, eds. Trout (The Wildlife Series). Stackpole Books. Harrisburg, PA.

Barko, V. A., and R. A. Hrabik. 2004. Abundance of Ohio Shrimp (*Macrobrachium ohione*) and Glass shrimp (*Palaemonetes kadiakensis*) in the unimpounded upper Mississippi River. American Midland Naturalist 151:265–273.

Brant, T. M. 1974. Effects of harvesting aquatic bait species from a small West Virginia Stream (part 1) and crayfish marking with florescent pigment (part 2). M.S. Thesis. Virginia Polytechnic Institute and State University. Blacksburg.

Butler, M. J., and R. A. Stein. 1985. An analysis of the mechanisms governing species replacements in crayfish. Oecologia 66:168–177.

Butler, R. S., R. J. DiStefano, and G. A. Schuster. 2003. Crayfish: an overlooked fauna. Endangered Species Bulletin 28:10–11.

Cooper, J. E. 2001. *Cambarus hobbsorum* (*Puncticambarus*), a new crayfish (Decapoda: Cambaridae) from North Carolina. Proceedings of the Biological Society of Washington 114:152–161.

Cooper, J. E. 2006a. A new species of crayfish of the genus *Cambarus* Erichson, 1846 (Decapoda:Cambaridae) from the eastern Blue Ridge foothills and western Piedmont Plateau of North Carolina. Proceedings of the Biological Society of Washington 119:67–80.

Cooper, J. E. 2006b. A new crayfish of the genus *Cambarus* Erichson, 1846, subgenus *Puncticambarus* Hobbs, 1969 (Decapoda:Cambaridae), from the Hiwassee River Basin of North Carolina. Proceedings of the Biological Society of Washington 119:81–90.

Cooper, J. E., and A. L. Braswell. 1995. Observations on North Carolina Crayfishes (Decapoda, Cambaridae). Brimleyana 22:87–132.

Cooper, J. E., and D. G. Cooper. 2003. A new crayfish of the genus *Cambarus* Erichson, 1846 (Decapoda: Cambaridae), from the Cape Fear River basin in the Sandhills of North Carolina. Proceedings of the Biological Society of Washington 116:920–932.

Corey, S. 1988. Comparative life histories of four populations of *Orconectes propinquus* (Girard, 1852) in Southwestern Ontario, Canada (Decapoda, Astacidea). Crustaceana 54:129–138.

Creed, R. P. 1994. Direct and indirect effects of crayfish grazing in a stream community. Ecology 75:2,091–2,103.

Creed, R. P., and J. M. Reed. 2004. Ecosystem engineering by crayfish in a headwater stream community. Journal of the North American Benthological Society 23:224–236.

DiStefano, R. J. 2000. Development of a quantitative sampling method to assess crayfish communities and macrohabitat associations in Missouri Ozarks streams. Missouri Department of Conservation. Dingell-Johnson Project F-1-R-42. Study S-41, Job 2. Final Report. Columbia, MO.

DiStefano, R. J., J. J. Decoske, T. M. Vangilder, and L. S. Barnes. 2003a. Macrohabitat partitioning among three crayfish species in two Missouri streams, U.S.A. Crustaceana 76:343–362.

DiStefano, R. J., C. M. Gale, B. A. Wagner, and R. D. Zweifel. 2003b. A sampling method to assess lotic crayfish communities. Journal of Crustacean Biology 23:678–690.

Eng, L. L., and R. A. Daniels. 1982. Life history, distribution, and status of *Pacifastacus fortis* (Decapoda: Astacidae). California Fish and Game 68:197–212.

Englund, G. 1999. Effects of fish on the local abundance of crayfish in stream pools. Oikos 87:48–56.

Englund, G., and J. J. Krupa. 2000. Habitat use by crayfish in stream pools: influence of predators, depth and body size. Freshwater Biology 43:75–83.

Faxon, W. 1884. Descriptions of a new species of *Cambarus*, to which is added a synonymic list of the known species of *Cambarus* and *Astacus*. Proceedings of the American Academy of Arts and Sciences 20:107–158.

Fenouil, E., and J. C. Chaix. 1985. Biological cycle and behavior of a population of *Austropotamobius pallipes*. Ecologia-Mediterranea 11:3–24.

Flinders, C. A., and D. D. Magoulick. 2005. Distribution, habitat use and life history of stream-dwelling crayfish in the spring river drainage of Arkansas and Missouri with a focus on the imperiled Mammoth Spring Crayfish (*Orconectes marchandi*). American Midland Naturalist 154:358–374.

Gore, J. A., and R. M. Bryant. 1990. Temporal shifts in physical habitat of the crayfish, *Orconectes neglectus* (Faxon). Hydrobiologia 199:131–142.

Hamr, P., and M. Berrill. 1985. The life histories of north-temperate populations of the crayfish *Cambarus robustus* and *Cambarus bartonii*. Canadian Journal of Zoology 63:2,313–2,322.

Hart, D. D. 1992. Community organization in streams: the importance of species interactions, physical factors, and chance. Oecologia 91:220–228.

Hobbs, H. H., Jr. 1969. On the distribution and phylogeny of the crayfish genus *Cambarus*, pp. 93–178. In, P. C. Holt, R. L. Hoffman, and C. W. Hart, eds. The Distributional History of the Biota of the Southern Appalachians, Part I: Invertebrates. Research Division Monograph 1. Virginia Polytechnic Institute and State University. Blacksburg, VA.

Hobbs, H. H., Jr. 1972. Crayfishes (Astacidae) of Northern and Middle America. U.S. Environmental Protection Agency Biota of Freshwater Ecosystems Identification Manual 9.

Hobbs, H. H., Jr. 1989. An illustrated checklist of the American crayfishes (Decapoda: Astacidae, Cambaridae, and Parastacidae). Smithsonian Contributions to Zoology No. 480.

Hobbs, H. H., Jr. and D. J. Peters. 1977. The entocytherid ostracods of North Carolina. Smithsonian Contributions to Zoology 247:1–73.

Hobbs, H. H., III. 2001. Decapoda. Pp. 955–1,001. *In* J. H. Thorpe, and A. P. Covich, eds. Ecology and Classification of North American Freshwater Invertebrates. Academic Press. San Diego, CA.

Hopkins, C. L. 1967. Systematics of the New Zealand freshwater crayfish *Paranephrops* (Crustacea: Decapoda: Parastacidea). New Zealand Journal of Marine and Freshwater Research 4:278–291.

Hulse, A. C., C. J. McCoy, and E. J. Censky. 2001. Amphibians and Reptiles of Pennsylvania and the Northeast. Cornell University. Ithaca, NY.

Huryn, A. D., and J. B. Wallace. 1987. Production and litter processing by crayfish in an Appalachian mountain stream. Freshwater Biology 18:277–286.

Jezerinac, R. F., G. W. Stocker, and D. C. Tarter. 1995. The Crayfishes (Decapoda: Cambaridae) of West Virginia. Ohio Biological Survey Bulletin New Series 10:1–193.

Jordan, F., K. J. Babbitt, C. C. McIvor, and S. J. Miller. 1996. Spatial ecology of the crayfish *Procambarus alleni* in a Florida wetland mosaic. Wetlands 16:134–142.

Jordan, S. M., R. M. Neumann, and E. T. Schultz. 2004. Distribution, habitat use, growth, and condition of a native and an introduced catfish species in the Hudson River estuary. Journal of Freshwater Ecology 19:59–67.

Kemp, S. J., and J. R. Spotila. 1997. Effects of urbanization on brown trout (*Salmo trutta*), other fishes and macroinvertebrates in Valley Creek, Valley Forge, Pennsylvania. American Midland Naturalist 139:55–68.

Lazzari, M. A., S. Sherman, and J. K. Kanwit. 2003. Nursery use of shallow habitats by epibenthic fishes in Maine nearshore waters. Estuarine coastal and Shelf Science 56:73–84.

Lieb, D. A., and R. F. Carline. 1999. The effects of urban runoff from a detention pond on the macroinvertebrate community of a headwater stream in central Pennsylvania. Journal of the Pennsylvania Academy of Science 73:99–105.

Lieb, D. A., and R. F. Carline. 2000. Effects of urban runoff from a detention pond on water quality, temperature, and caged *Gammarus minus* (Say) (Amphipoda) in a headwater stream. Hydrobiologia 441:107–116.

Lieb, D. A., R. F. Carline, and H. M. Ingram. 2007. Status of Native and Invasive Crayfish in Ten National Park Service Properties in Pennsylvania. Technical Report NPS/NER/NRTR—2007/085. National Park Service. Philadelphia, PA.

Lodge, D. M., C. A. Taylor, D. M. Holdich, and J. Skurdal. 2000. Nonindigenous crayfish threaten North American freshwater biodiversity: lessons from Europe. Fisheries 25:7–20.

Mendenhall, W., and R. J. Beaver. 1994. Introduction to Probability and Statistics. Duxbury Press. Belmont, CA.

Meredith, W. G., and F. J. Schwartz. 1960. Maryland crayfishes. Maryland Department of Research Education, Educational Series 46. 32 p.

Nyström, P., P. Stenroth, N. Holmqvist, O. Berglund, P. Larsson, and W. Graneli. 2006. Crayfish in lakes and streams: individual and population responses to predation, productivity and substratum availability. Freshwater Biology 51:2,096–2,113.

Ortmann, A. E. 1906. The crawfishes of the state of Pennsylvania. Memoirs of the Carnegie Museum 2:343–523.

Ott, R. L. 1992. An Introduction to Statistical Methods and Data Analysis. Duxbury Press. Belmont, CA.

Page, L. M. 1985. The Crayfishes and Shrimps (Decapoda) of Illinois. Illinois Natural History Survey Bulletin 33:335–446.

Platts, W. S., W. F. Megahan, and G. W. Minshall. 1983. Methods for evaluating stream, riparian, and biotic conditions. U.S. Forest Service General Technical Report INT-138.

Pursiainen, M., M. Saarela, and K. Westman. 1987. Molting and growth of the noble crayfish, *Astacus astacus*, in an oligotrophic lake. Freshwater Crayfish 7:155–64.

Rabeni, C. F. 1985. Resource partitioning by stream-dwelling crayfish: the influence of body size. American Midland Naturalist 113:20–29.

Rabeni, C. F., K. J. Collier., S. M. Parkyn, and B. J. Hicks. 1997. Evaluating techniques for sampling stream crayfish (*Paranephrops planifrons*). New Zealand Journal of Marine and Freshwater Research 31:693–700.

Rabeni, C. F., M. Gossett, and D. D. McClendon. 1995. Contribution of crayfish to benthic invertebrate production and trophic ecology of an Ozark stream. Freshwater Crayfish 10:163–173.

Reynolds, J. D. 2002. Growth and reproduction. Pp. 152–191. *In* D. M. Holdich, ed. Biology of Freshwater Crayfish. Blackwell Science Publishing. Oxford, UK.

Richardson, A. J., and R. A. Cook. 2006. Habitat use by caridean shrimps in lowland rivers. Marine and Freshwater Research 57:695–701.

Riggert, C. M., R. J. DiStefano, and D. B. Noltie. 1999. Distributions and selected aspects of the life histories and habitat associations of the crayfishes *Orconectes peruncus* (Creaser, 1931) and *O. quadruncus* (Creaser, 1933) in Missouri. American Midland Naturalist 142:348–362.

Schofield, K. A., C. M. Pringle, J. L. Meyer, and A. B. Sutherland. 2001. The importance of crayfish in the breakdown of rhododendron leaf litter. Freshwater Biology 46: 1,191–1,204.

Schwartz, F. J., and W. G. Meredith. 1960. Crayfishes of the Cheat River watershed, West Virginia and Pennsylvania. Part I. Species and localities. Ohio Journal of Science 60:40–54.

Skurdal, J., and T. Qvenild. 1986. Growth, maturity and fecundity of *Astacus astacus* in Lake Steinsfjorden, S.E. Norway. Freshwater Crayfish 6:182–186.

Sloto, R. A. 1990. Geohydrology and simulation of ground-water flow in the carbonate rocks of the Valley Creek basin, Eastern Chester County, Pennsylvania. USGS Water-resources Investigations Report 89-4169. 60 pp.

Smith, G. R. T., F. M. Learner., F. Slater, and J. Foster. 1996. Habitat features important for the conservation of the native crayfish *Austropotamobius pallipes* in Britain. Biological Conservation 75:239–246.

Steel, R. G. D., and J. H. Torrie. 1980. Principles and Procedures of Statistics a Biometrical Approach. McGraw-Hill Book Company. New York, NY.

Steffy, L. Y., and S. S. Kilham. 2004. Elevated $\delta^{15}N$ in stream biota in areas with septic tank systems in an urban watershed. Ecological Applications 14:637–641.

Stenroth, P., and P. Nyström. 2003. Exotic crayfish in a brown water stream: effects on juvenile trout, invertebrates and algae. Freshwater Biology 48:466–475.

Taylor, C. A., and G. A. Schuster. 2004. The Crayfishes of Kentucky. Illinois Natural History Survey Special Publication No. 28. viii + 219 pp.

Taylor, C. A., M. L. Warren, J. F. Fitzpatrick, H. H. Hobbs, III., R. F. Jezerinac., W. L. Pflieger, and H. W. Robison. 1996. Conservation Status of Crayfishes of the United States and Canada. Fisheries 21:25–38.

Taylor, R. C. 1983. Drought-induced changes in crayfish populations along a stream continuum. American Midland Naturalist 110:286–298.

Usio, N. 2000. Effects of crayfish on leaf processing and invertebrate colonization of leaves in a headwater stream: decoupling of a trophic cascade. Oecologia 124:608–614.

Van Den Brink, F. W. B., G. Van Der Velde, and J. F. M. Geelen. 1988. Life history parameters and temperature-related activity of an American crayfish *Orconectes limosus* (Rafinesque) (Crustacea: Decapoda) in the area of the major rivers in the Netherlands. Archiv-fuer-Hydrobiologie 114:275–290.

Wallace, E. M., and K. J. Hartman. 2006. Habitat utilization and movement patterns of sub-harvestable largemouth bass (*Micropterus salmoides*) in the Ohio River. Journal of Freshwater Ecology 21:663–672.

Westhoff, J. T., J. A. Guyot, and R. J. DiStefano. 2006. Distribution of the imperiled Williams' crayfish (*Orconectes williamsi*) in the White River drainage of Missouri: Associations with multi-scale environmental variables. American Midland Naturalist 156:273–288.

Westman, K., O. Sumari, and M. Pursiainen. 1978. Electric fishing in sampling crayfish. Freshwater Crayfish 4:251–256.

Zar, J. H. 1999. Biostatistical Analysis. Prentice-Hall, Inc. Upper Saddle River, NJ.

As the nation's primary conservation agency, the Department of the Interior has responsibility for most of our nationally owned public land and natural resources. This includes fostering sound use of our land and water resources; protecting our fish, wildlife, and biological diversity; preserving the environmental and cultural values of our national parks and historical places; and providing for the enjoyment of life through outdoor recreation. The department assesses our energy and mineral resources and works to ensure that their development is in the best interests of all our people by encouraging stewardship and citizen participation in their care. The department also has a major responsibility for American Indian reservation communities and for people who live in island territories under U.S. administration.

NPS D-095 June 2007